THE WELLINGTON ARCH
AND
THE MARBLE ARCH

Steven Brindle and David Robi

Usually built to commemorate a great victory, the triumphal arch was a familiar feature of the Roman world. In the 1820s, this classical model was adapted by two of the finest architects of the day: Decimus Burton used it for his arch at Green Park, later known as the Wellington Arch, and John Nash copied the Arch of Constantine in Rome as the basis for the Marble Arch. This was no mere accident, since both arches were indeed meant to serve as victory monuments. After much public lobbying, Britain was at last to have appropriate memorials marking its military and naval triumphs over Napoleonic France.

The patron behind these works was King George IV, who had long been greatly interested in architecture. His vision was that of a grand ceremonial route into his newly planned metropolitan residence, Buckingham Palace. The Wellington Arch would serve as the outer entrance at the top of Constitution Hill, and the Marble Arch would open gloriously into the courtyard of the palace itself.

This guidebook explores the context for the design and construction of each arch, and explains their turbulent later histories, including their complete removal to fresh sites in the Victorian era, through to the present day.

❖ CONTENTS ❖

PUBLIC RECORD OFFICE

Published by English Heritage
1 Waterhouse Square, 138–142 Holborn, London EC1N 2ST
www.english-heritage.org.uk
© English Heritage 2001
First published by English Heritage 2001, revised reprint 2009
Photographs by English Heritage Photographic Unit
and copyright of English Heritage, unless otherwise stated

Edited by Julia Wigg
Designed by Pauline Hull
Plans by Philip Winton and Richard Morris
Printed in England by Park Communications
C30, 05/09, 00001, ISBN 978 1 85074 794 9

Decimus Burton's design for a capital on the Wellington Arch

ARCHES OF TRIUMPH

London's West End is embellished with two handsome triumphal arches, the Wellington Arch and the Marble Arch. To a remarkable extent, the stories of these well-known metropolitan landmarks have run in parallel. Both were planned in 1825 and built about 1826–30, and both were designed to commemorate Britain's victories over Napoleonic France. They were conceived as grand entrances to Buckingham Palace: the Wellington Arch (then usually called the Green Park Arch) forming an outer gateway to Constitution Hill, whereas the Marble Arch was to stand at the very front of the palace courtyard. This is not at all apparent today, due to the extraordinary subsequent histories of the two monuments.

Both arches were caught up in the unhappy public row over the rebuilding of George IV's Buckingham Palace. Although the Green Park Arch was completed, most of its intended ornament was left out as an economy measure. The Marble Arch was only ever built in a much reduced form, with almost all of its sculpture ending up elsewhere. Subsequently, the Green Park Arch was taken over as the base for a gigantic equestrian statue of the Duke of Wellington, erected in 1846 in circumstances of extreme controversy. Then, in 1882, it fell victim to a road-widening scheme. It was moved to its present site looking down Constitution Hill, losing the statue in the process, but retaining the

The north face of the Marble Arch, looking towards Hyde Park

name 'Wellington Arch'. In 1912 it was adorned with a magnificent sculpture of a quadriga (four-horse chariot). Meanwhile, the Marble Arch had been removed to its present position in 1850–51, and in 1908 it too was seriously affected by road improvements. The situation was made still worse by the drastic Hyde Park Lane highway engineering of 1960–62, works which left both arches completely isolated on vast traffic islands. Consequently, neither monument resembles its creator's original design, and both have long been robbed of their intended settings.

In 1999, the arches passed into the care of English Heritage. Since then, major repairs have been carried out to the Wellington Arch, which has been adapted for public access with viewing platforms over the porticoes and internal exhibition spaces. The Marble Arch is currently not open to the public on a regular basis; its interiors are too small and the access stairs too restricted. However, the histories of these two arches of triumph are so closely linked, and they are both of such interest, that it would hardly be appropriate to consider one without the other.

The Duke of Wellington's funeral procession, 1852, passing beneath the Wellington Arch

GUILDHALL LIBRARY/BRIDGEMAN ART LIBRARY

THE WELLINGTON ARCH

The 'western entrance' to London

In the mid-eighteenth century London's new 'West End' was spreading rapidly outwards through Mayfair and St Marylebone. The old city boundaries had been left far behind: Temple Bar on the Strand, for long the western boundary of the City, could no longer be regarded as the entrance to London. Where, then, did the newer London begin? The largest obstacle to its westward expansion was Hyde Park; this was flanked by the Oxford road to the north and the Kensington turnpike road to the south. The Oxford road was blemished by the public gallows at Tyburn (the present site of the Marble Arch), where London's convicted criminals had long been hanged. Perhaps for this reason, the idea emerged that Hyde Park Corner, where the Kensington road met Piccadilly, was the most plausible candidate as the new 'western entrance'.

The tollgate and lodges at Hyde Park Corner at the end of the eighteenth century

*Robert Adam's design for
an arch at Hyde Park
Corner, 1778*

*John Soane's design for a
triumphal entrance to
London, 1826*

The West End was planned and built by private developers, not by the state, so it was characteristic that for many Georgian travellers, their first sight of London was the simple wooden tollgate at Hyde Park Corner, operated by the Kensington Turnpike Trust. A number of architects produced speculative designs for grand city gates here, including Robert Adam, Jeffry Wyatt and John Soane, but the government was unwilling to pay for such extravagant monuments. All that happened was a rebuilding of the tollgate and lodges in a simple but dignified style, about 1791, to designs by Henry Holland.

After the Napoleonic Wars, many people supported the idea of a national monument to commemorate Britain's victories, and in 1816 Parliament voted £300,000 for the purpose. The Prince Regent, afterwards King George IV, was greatly interested in architecture, supporting several grand building projects, notably Regent's Park, Regent Street, and the rebuilding of the British Museum. However,

the proposed victory monument was much slower to get off the ground. Several ideas were put forward, but the one which seems to have commanded most support was a victory arch doubling as a western entrance at Hyde Park Corner. The official architect, John Soane, produced several such designs between 1817 and 1826, amid a remarkable series of proposals for a triumphal 'royal route' from Knightsbridge, via a new palace in Green Park, to a rebuilt Westminster.

Soane's triumphal route was the grandest and most coherent of the master plans being promoted in these years, but he was to be disappointed, for George IV's thinking developed in another direction. In the early 1820s the king was planning to remodel his parents' private residence, Buckingham House. He did not give the job to Soane (who had a claim to it), but presented it to John Nash, a rather more compliant figure. It was agreed that the national victory monument should be a triumphal arch, based on the Arch of Constantine in Rome, and that it should be located in front of the new palace: this developed into the Marble Arch. At Hyde Park Corner, instead of a grand western entrance, the king and his advisers proposed to have a pair of gates into Hyde Park and Green Park, facing each other across Piccadilly, the latter doubling as an outer gate to Buckingham Palace.

Decimus Burton and Hyde Park Corner: 1825–30

In the summer of 1825, the Office of Woods and Forests – which was responsible for maintaining London's royal parks – instructed its architect Decimus Burton to prepare designs for a pair of grand park entrances at Hyde Park Corner. Burton was already at work on a series of gates, lodges and railings around Hyde Park, which is undoubtedly why he was chosen for the job. However, this was no ordinary commission: the idea almost certainly originated from George IV and his circle of friends, notably Sir Charles Long, later Lord Farnborough. In 1828, Burton told a parliamentary committee that he had taken instructions for Hyde Park Corner from a group of 'five or six noblemen and gentlemen', generally including Lord Liverpool (the Prime Minister), Lord Goderich (Chancellor of the Exchequer), Robert Peel (Home Secretary), J C Herries (Financial Secretary to the Treasury), and Lord Farnborough, as well as Charles Arbuthnot, Secretary of the Office of Woods and Forests.

In August 1825, Burton presented his first designs to this exalted committee. His design for a 'façade' to Hyde Park is identical to the screen as built: this was personally approved

Decimus Burton's first design for the Green Park arch, 1825

❖ DECIMUS BURTON (1800–81) ❖

Decimus Burton was the tenth son (hence his name) of James Burton, one of the greatest Georgian builder-developers. Decimus left Tonbridge School in 1816 and started work as an assistant to his father. His first known design was the new Burton family house, The Holme, on the Inner Circle of Regent's Park (1817–18), followed by South Villa, Regent's Park (1818), Cornwall Terrace (1821) and Clarence Terrace (1823). All of these were built by his father following John Nash's master plan for the park.

Burton was very industrious: he worked on a number of town-planning projects, including the Calverley Estate in Tunbridge Wells (from 1828) and Fleetwood

Decimus Burton as a young man

in Lancashire (from 1836). Although he designed a number of Gothic buildings (including several churches), their detail is dry and repetitive, and it is difficult to think that his heart was in them. His finest works are neo-classical,

such as the Athenaeum Club on Pall Mall (1827–30), Grimston Park in Yorkshire (1840) and his work at the Royal Botanic Gardens in Kew (1845–48). Burton owned a large collection of plaster casts of classical ornament, which undoubtedly informed his work and which he left to the South Kensington Museum (now the Victoria and Albert Museum). He took great pains over designing his classical decoration; the full-size detail drawings for the Wellington Arch are wonderful pieces of draughtsmanship. Burton was successful and busy until the taste for neo-classicism was overtaken by the Gothic Revival, and his career seems to have faltered about 1855. He died, a wealthy man, in 1881.

by the king with the initials 'GR'. Burton proposed that the gateway to Green Park opposite should replicate the centre of the Hyde Park Screen. The committee did not think this was grand enough, saying that as the Green Park Arch was intended to 'form one of the Approaches to the Palace, it would be respectful to His Majesty to have it upon a Scale and of a Character more ornamental than that of the Façade opposite'.

So Burton produced a second design for a magnificent single-opening triumphal arch, with Corinthian columns rather than the simpler Ionic ones he was proposing to use on the screen. He made a superb presentation watercolour showing the arch and screen together, covered in rich ornament celebrating Britain's victories over the French. There were to be trophies of arms, statues of guardsmen, a frieze of horsemen around the attic of the arch, and a sculpture of a quadriga on top. The second design was accepted in November. Burton was hard at work on the detailed drawings in January 1826, and in May his estimate for the

Opposite: Decimus Burton's design for a screen entrance to Hyde Park, 1825

Below: Decimus Burton's second design for the arch, watercolour perspective, 1826

So the scaffolding came down, Burton's arch was left without most of its decoration, and has remained in that state ever since.

The arch's general form derives from ancient examples such as the Arch of Titus in Rome, or the Arch of Trajan at Benevento, but there is no close model for Burton's design. Indeed, it could not have been built in ancient times: the broad lintels spanning the central openings could never have been executed in load-bearing masonry. They were spanned with girders made of cast and wrought iron, exploiting Britain's new industrial technology; the stone lintel blocks are suspended from the girders with iron rods.

Decimus Burton's second design for the Green Park arch, elevations

Detail of Burton's architrave design for the arch

Right: detail of the Wellington Arch gates, designed by Burton and cast in iron by Joseph Bramah & Sons in Pimlico, for 1,700 guineas. The gates have been restored to their original bronze-green colour

arch (£18,891 6s. 0d. not including sculpture) was accepted by the Treasury.

The arch and screen rose together, and in 1828 the screen was nearing completion; John Henning junior carved a version of the Panathenaic procession, from the Elgin Marbles, on its central attic. The carcass of the arch was almost complete, and Burton wrote to the Treasury urging that the sculptural decoration be 'executed forthwith' while the building was still scaffolded, it being common practice for such ornament to be carved *in situ*. But the costs had already risen to around £21,000, and Burton thought the carved trophies and friezes would amount to another £5,695. Eventually, in January 1830, the Treasury refused: Buckingham Palace had run wildly over budget and was far from complete. Further spending on the arch would not be sanctioned until this was sorted out.

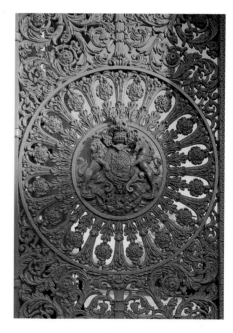

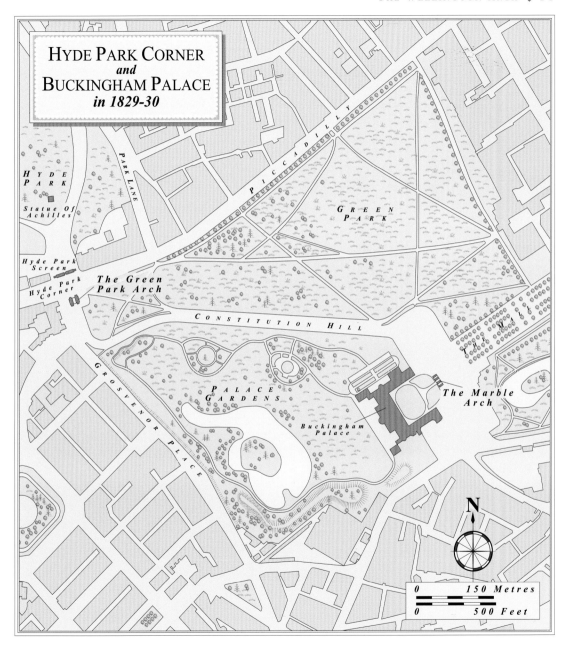

HYDE PARK CORNER
and
BUCKINGHAM PALACE
in 1829-30

HYDE
PARK

Statue Of
Achilles

PARK LANE

PICCADILLY

GREEN
PARK

Hyde Park
Screen

Hyde Park
Corner

The Green
Park Arch

CONSTITUTION HILL

THE MALL

GROSVENOR PLACE

PALACE
GARDENS

Buckingham
Palace

The Marble
Arch

N

0   150 Metres

0   500 Feet

Westmacott's statue of Achilles, Hyde Park

Matthew Cotes Wyatt's design for strengthening works to support the Wellington statue, 1846

The Wellington Memorial

After 1815, Britain saw several projects to honour Arthur Wellesley, the first Duke of Wellington, the nation's greatest living hero. A committee of 'Ladies of England' raised subscriptions and commissioned the great nude statue of Achilles by Richard Westmacott, which was erected close to Hyde Park Corner and to Apsley House, the Duke's London residence, in 1822. However, it was not until 1838 that a National Memorial Committee of sixty-two worthies was formed. It was dominated by an inner clique, led by the fifth Duke of Rutland, John Wilson Croker MP and Colonel Frederick Trench MP, who seem to have been determined from the start to impose their own views.

Like the 'Ladies of England', they thought it would be complimentary to

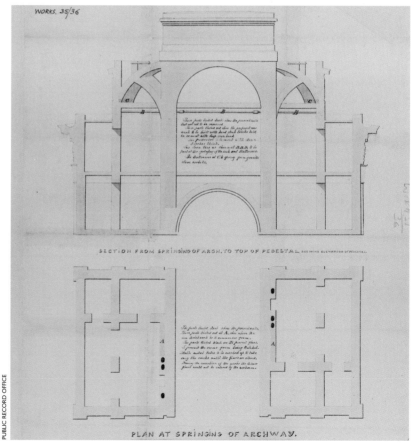

AWFUL APPARITION TO A GENTLEMAN, WHILST SHAVING, IN THE
EDGWARE ROAD.—*Sept.* 29, 1846.

the Duke of Wellington to place the
memorial close to Apsley House.
Croker and the Duke of Rutland
formed the idea of using the
incomplete Green Park Arch as a base
for their monument, and by exploiting
his contacts with the government
Rutland achieved royal assent for this
in June 1838. Next, he sprang the
choice of an artist on a thinly attended
meeting of his committee and secured
the nomination of his protégé Matthew
Cotes Wyatt, who had worked for
him at Belvoir Castle, Leicestershire.
When the other members of the
committee found out, they reacted
angrily, and there was a public row.

However, this was overshadowed by
the row which broke out when Wyatt's
design became publicly known. He
and Rutland had conceived the idea
of erecting a giant bronze equestrian
statue of the Duke of Wellington –

at 8.5 metres (28 feet) high the largest
equestrian figure ever made – on top
of Burton's arch. Most people thought
that the statue and the arch would
be completely disproportionate to
each other, and the design attracted
vehement criticism. Nevertheless, the
Duke of Rutland would not budge,
and Wyatt was ordered to proceed.
Matters went relatively quiet for the
six years which it took him to make
the colossal statue, in a studio in
Paddington. It took over 100 tonnes
of casting plaster and 40 tonnes of
bronze, most of it from captured
French cannon, and cost £30,000.
The horse is so big that a man on
horseback could ride under its belly.

In 1845, as the statue neared
completion, the row broke out
again with renewed vigour.
Decimus Burton was asked
to cooperate with Wyatt
in preparing the arch to
receive this huge and
unexpected ornament.
Burton, who had never
been consulted about this
use of his building, was
appalled, and complained
bitterly to Lord Lincoln,
the Chief Commissioner
of Woods and Forests.
Burton was not alone:
the hostile voices, led by
Punch and *The Builder*,
were in a large majority,
and the House of Commons
united to condemn the design.

Cartoons from Punch,
September 1846

THE PROPOSED STATUE OF THE IRON DUKE.

ARTHUR WELLESLEY, ❖ DUKE OF WELLINGTON ❖ (1769–1852)

Arthur Wellesley, the future Duke of Wellington, was the fourth son of the first Earl of Mornington, an Anglo-Irish landowner. Marked out for a military career at an early stage, he was educated at Eton and at the French military academy at Angers. Commissioned as a lieutenant in 1792, he served against the French revolutionary army in the Netherlands in 1794–95. Between 1797 and 1805 he commanded British forces in India, gaining victory against a succession of enemies, and returning to Britain with a reputation as a formidable commander.

In 1808 Wellesley was made a lieutenant-general and given command of an expedition to protect Portugal against French invasion. The 'Peninsular War' of 1808–14 went through a series of dramatic reversals of fortune. Wellesley was severely tried by the inability of the government to support his forces consistently, but

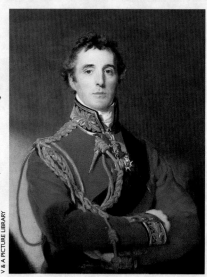

V & A PICTURE LIBRARY

Portrait of the Duke of Wellington by Sir Thomas Lawrence

he received personal recognition, being created Earl of Wellington in 1812. In May 1813 Wellington began his final victorious campaign, defeating the French at Vitoria and driving them back over the Pyrenees, to capture Toulouse in April 1814. He was made Duke of Wellington in 1814.

Wellington was at the Congress of Vienna when Napoleon made his sudden return from exile to France, in March 1815. Sent to respond to this new threat with Anglo-Hanoverian and Dutch forces, he faced Napoleon and a slightly larger French army at Waterloo (south of Brussels) on 18 June 1815. Waterloo, one of the most dramatic and hard-fought battles in history, was won with the help of Prussian forces under Marshal Blücher, but at dreadful cost and by a slender margin, 'the nearest run thing you ever saw in your life', as Wellington himself put it. Later he served in government and as a diplomat in several roles, notably as Prime Minister, 1828–30. Revered as Britain's greatest commander and pre-eminent elder statesman, he was in 1817 given the estate of Stratfield Saye in Hampshire as a token of the nation's gratitude, and bought Apsley House at Hyde Park Corner with funds voted by Parliament.

Sir Robert Peel's government was becoming uneasy, and offered the Memorial Committee other sites for the statue, such as Horse Guards or Waterloo Place, but the Duke of Rutland refused to compromise. At length, on 5 August 1846, Lord Morpeth revoked Queen Victoria's permission of 1838. It was, perhaps, unfortunate that the government waited until the Memorial Committee had spent a lot of money adapting the arch before finally nerving itself to say no. It then felt embarrassed and backed down, allowing the statue to be erected for a three-week trial period.

On 27 September 1846, the giant statue was taken on a special car drawn by twenty-nine horses, accompanied by a grand military parade, to Hyde Park Corner. When lifted into place, the statue was greeted with gales of derisive and hostile criticism. Lord Morpeth told the Memorial Committee that the government 'were not enabled to think the effect favourable either to the statue or the arch', and asked for it to come down again. However, it was the Duke of Wellington himself who finally ended the debate. He had maintained a dignified silence throughout these rather undignified proceedings.

The Wellington Arch and statue, about 1860

Now he privately indicated to the new Prime Minister, Lord John Russell, that he would regard the removal of the statue as a humiliating mark of royal displeasure, and would feel obliged to resign all of his official commissions (which included Commander-in-Chief of the army). Faced with this ultimatum, the government caved in. After nine years of bitter argument, the Duke of Rutland won his point and the statue stayed, in circumstances verging on farce. Historic views make it clear why the statue attracted such dislike: it is stiffly composed and oddly proportioned; it was also completely disproportionate to the arch.

The arch moved: 1882–83

Hyde Park Corner had long suffered from heavy traffic, and after the opening of Victoria Station in 1860 this grew much worse. In 1880 a new Liberal government came to power, and the First Commissioner of Works, Shaw Lefevre, took up a scheme to widen the roads and create a new highway cutting the corner between Piccadilly and Grosvenor Place. This would involve dismantling the Wellington Arch, and the Office of Works proposed to move it a short distance, to look down Constitution Hill.

The arch before dismantling, 1883

HASTINGS MUSEUM AND ART GALLERY

In 1883 the arch was dismantled and reconstructed on its present site. The Wellington statue was taken down in the process, and the question of what to do with it arose again. No one seems to have wanted it back on the arch, and a strongly worded memorandum from the president and academicians of the Royal Academy urged the government to relieve London of 'a blot which has long been a source of annoyance to Englishmen and of derision to foreigners'. A committee chaired by the Prince of Wales was formed to consider the beautification of the newly formed place. It cast around for another site for the giant statue, but not finding one that met with approval proposed to melt it down. At this point the army spoke up; much of the money subscribed for the statue had come from officers, and they wanted it if no one else did. So, in 1885, the statue was unveiled on a new site near the garrison church at Aldershot by the Prince of Wales, where it remains. The committee commissioned Sir Joseph Boehm to make a new equestrian statue of the Duke of Wellington, and in 1888 the very fine monument which stands opposite Apsley House was unveiled.

Cartoon from Punch, *July 1883*

Hyde Park Corner and the Wellington Arch, about 1890

Boehm's statue of Wellington

Below: H M Office of Works, unexecuted design for gates to flank the arch, 1906

In 1901 the architect Aston Webb won the competition for a national memorial to Queen Victoria. The result was the landscaping of the Mall and the splendid public space in front of Buckingham Palace, around Sir Thomas Brock's marble monument. In 1906 Webb was asked to present designs for Constitution Hill and the Wellington Arch, to draw them into this ceremonial landscape. Webb had the hill widened and designed handsome gate-piers flanking the arch, emphasising its role as an outer entrance to Buckingham Palace.

Adrian Jones and the quadriga

In 1891 the Prince of Wales, later Edward VII, attended the Royal Academy's annual banquet. He noticed there a splendid plaster sculpture called 'Triumph', representing a chariot pulled by four wildly rearing horses and driven by a boy, who in his concentration has not seen the tall, winged figure of Peace landing behind him. This original and spirited group was by Captain Adrian Jones. The prince remembered the Wellington Arch, and thought that a larger version of Jones' sculpture would be the ideal ornament with which to complete it. He sent for Jones, who was enthusiastic about the idea, but there was no money to carry it out and matters moved slowly. The Office of Works was consulted, and in 1899 Jones produced scaled designs and an estimate of £15,615 for making the quadriga, including £6,000 for his work for three years and £7,000 for casting it in bronze. At last, in 1907, the Royal Household found a suitably discreet donor in the banker Herbert Stern, recently created Lord Michelham of Hellingly. The donation seems not to have covered the whole cost; the government was certainly not going to make up the difference, and by Jones' account he agreed to make it for 'a sum which was quite inadequate', effectively subsidising it himself.

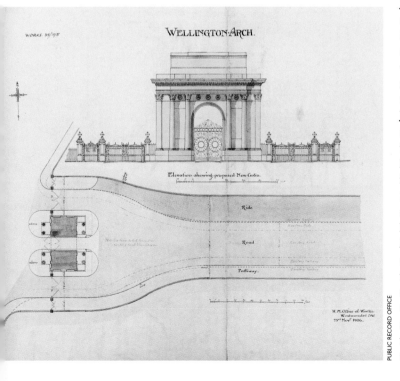

WELLINGTON ARCH.

Elevation shewing proposed New Gates.

❖ ADRIAN JONES (1845–1938) ❖

Adrian Jones was born in Ludlow. His early love of country life and the natural world was combined with a love of painting, but his father opposed his desire to become an artist, urging him to join the army instead. Adrian proposed a compromise, that he should train as a vet and join the cavalry in that capacity. In January 1867 he was gazetted, joining the Royal Horse Artillery at Ahmednagar in India. He served as a veterinary captain for twenty-three years. Throughout his army career he produced sketches and paintings of dogs and horses for his army and sporting friends. Encouraged by a sculptor friend, C B Birch, he took up small-scale figure sculpture, and in 1884 exhibited his first bronze at the Royal Academy.

By the time Jones retired from the army in 1889, he had established a successful second career, and took a studio in Chelsea. When the Prince of Wales suggested a large-scale version of his group 'Triumph' be

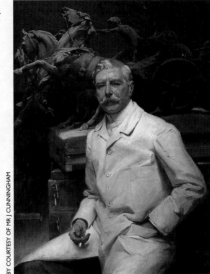

Portrait of Adrian Jones by Alfred Priest

BY COURTESY OF MR J CUNNINGHAM

made for the Wellington Arch, Jones visited the President of the Royal Academy, Sir Frederic Leighton, to seek his support. Leighton was unhelpful, questioning Jones' ability to produce a heroically-scaled piece. Jones responded to this challenge with 'Duncan's Horses', a remarkable group of three fighting stallions (1892). This dramatic composition aroused great admiration, but also led to ugly

and false rumours that Jones had not made it himself. Jones was enraged by the incident, which increased his sense of isolation from the artistic establishment.

His career prospered anyway, notably with a commission from the Prince of Wales for a life-size sculpture of his horse, Persimmon (1895), which still stands at Sandringham House. Jones produced several more large-scale monuments, including the Royal Marines Memorial on the Mall (1902), the Duke of Cambridge statue on Whitehall (1907), and the Cavalry Memorial in Hyde Park (1924). Most of his work, though, continued to be on a smaller scale: paintings and bronzes of horses and dogs.

Jones was never an avant-garde figure, but the English love of sporting art and the high quality of his work kept the commissions coming well into the 1920s. The quadriga is his great masterpiece. Jones was keenly aware of this, subsidising the making of it himself, and devoting a chapter to it in his autobiography.

Adrian Jones' original sculptural group 'Triumph'

Below: Jones, his assistants, and the clay model of a horse

Below right: Jones and his assistants having tea inside the plaster mould of a horse

Opposite: the finished quadriga and the foundry workers

In 1908 Jones started work in his studio in Chelsea. The composition was so big that he had to model one element at a time, and could only judge the total effect when it was finished. Each horse began with a metal armature, covered with timber framing, on which Jones built up modelling clay (each clay horse weighed 7 tonnes, while Peace and the chariot were even heavier), referring always to his sketches and models, and having 'constant recourse to callipers'. When each figure was complete, Jones would summon Italian specialists in plaster-casting to construct a mould in coloured plaster around it, in sections. These were pulled away, destroying the clay original. The mould was assembled in sections, and a full

plaster cast made. Jones took three years to model the whole group, and received several visits from King Edward VII; by the time of the last royal visit in 1910, the modelling was complete, but the bronze-casting had only just begun. 'I am sorry', said the king, 'for I shall never see it'. He died a few weeks later.

The plaster casts were taken to A B Burton & Company at Thames Ditton, one of the leading bronze statuary foundries in Britain. Each figure was made in several pieces by the lengthy process of sand-casting, each horse being cast in seven pieces. The quadriga is a large and complex structure, around 8.8 metres (29 feet) high and weighing 38 tonnes. It would have to be structurally stable and withstand the worst of the weather.

This presented a technical challenge, and Jones and Burton retained a consulting engineer, Alexander Drew, who designed the steel roof-frame to carry the quadriga, and its internal supporting framework. The quadriga has remained stable for eighty-eight years, and, despite its exposed position, it remains in very good condition.

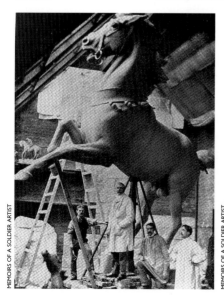

ELMBRIDGE MUSEUM

In the summer of 1911 the casting
was completed, and the quadriga was
trial-assembled next to the foundry.
The group was dismantled again and
taken to Hyde Park Corner, where it
was erected on the arch in January
1912. Adrian Jones had planned a
'most original and ingenious scheme'
for unveiling his composition, but
neither the Office of Works nor the
Royal Household were interested in
paying for this. Instead, King George
V and Queen Mary drove to view the
quadriga on 2 April 1912, and Jones,
Burton, and Lord Michelham were
presented to them.

*Above: sections of the
quadriga being moved
in 1911*

Right: the restored quadriga

THE
MARBLE ARCH

Buckingham Palace origins: 1825–50

The Prince Regent first began to consider moving from Carlton House to his parents' private residence, Buckingham House, in 1818. Lord Liverpool warned against it, saying that £150,000 was the 'utmost sum' which might be found from the public purse. The prince believed nothing worthwhile could be achieved for less than £450,000. In the event, nothing was done. Even after George's accession to the throne in 1820, it took time for the plan to mature, but in 1825 Parliament finally passed a bill which allowed for part of the Crown land revenues to be applied to the 'repair and improvement' of Buckingham House. The way was at last open.

The king's favoured architect, John Nash, had already made some preliminary plans, but he had also been trying to persuade his patron to build on a different site. The king would have none of it: he was too old to build a new palace, yet he 'must have a *pied-à-terre*' which had to be located at Buckingham House because of the 'early associations' which endeared him to the spot. Nash resigned himself to the king's wishes.

The plaster model of about 1826, showing Nash's original scheme of decoration. This was to be the military face of the arch. The attic plinth, the section immediately below the equestrian statue, has been accidentally reversed: Britannia was intended to surmount the naval face of the arch

The scale of the conversion, however, and the speed with which it had to press ahead to satisfy royal impatience were eventually to prove his undoing. Work began in June 1825, before the land revenue bill, or even an estimate of costs, had been laid before Parliament. Within a week there were nearly 400 men employed on the site.

Very few of Nash's drawings for Buckingham Palace survive, so it is impossible to be sure if a triumphal entrance arch was a component of his design from the beginning. He was possibly influenced by a contemporary suggestion made by Sir William Hillary MP: that there might be no better memorial to the nation's victories in the Napoleonic Wars than a triumphal monument, modelled on the Arch of Constantine in Rome (AD 315), and placed so as 'to form the grand approach to the future royal residence of the British capital'. In any case Nash was to take up just such an idea, positioning his arch at the east front of the new palace

Buckingham Palace with the Marble Arch in its original location: a watercolour by Joseph Nash, 1846

courtyard and linking it to projecting wings by decorative railings. In devising this scheme, however, there is no doubt that the example of the Arc de Triomphe du Carrousel (1806–08) in Paris – built as an entrance to the Tuileries palace by Napoleon himself, and seen by Nash in 1814 – was also very much in the architect's mind.

For the details of his arch, Nash was to collaborate with the eminent neo-classical sculptor, John Flaxman. Fortunately, a wonderful little plaster model survives to demonstrate just what they had in mind. Like the Arch of Constantine in Rome, and the Carrousel in Paris, the Buckingham Palace arch was to be of the Corinthian order, with the same triple-arched elevation, and similarly adorned with commemorative sculpture. The sculpture programme itself was to be evenly divided between the naval and military themes. One side and one end was allotted to the army, principally the battle of Waterloo; the opposite faces were to feature the navy, concentrating on the battle of Trafalgar. There was to be an attic pedestal above the central arch, adorned with reliefs on the principal façades, and surmounted with an equestrian statue of the king.

Initially, the arch was to be built of Bath stone, the material Nash had chosen for the external palace works. But early in 1826 the decision was taken to clad the entire structure in

marble. Nash had already sent Joseph Browne, a respected marble dealer and worker, to Carrara in Tuscany to buy as much of the material as he could for the decorative interiors of the palace. In sourcing further quantities for the arch, it was Browne who suggested using 'ordinary marble', a dense grey-white type of Carrara known as 'Ravaccione'.

At long last, construction of 'the Marble Arch' began towards the end of 1827, with Nash content to leave much to Browne's care. By February 1828 the foundations were complete and the massive marble slabs had been set around the base plinth, though already there were ugly clouds gathering over the palace works as a whole. Parliament was showing increasing anxiety over the total expenditure, and the building

Above: an 1829 cartoon depicting John Bull confronting Nash with the enormous bill for the palace and arch

Below: Nash's Marble Arch was almost certainly modelled on the Arch of Constantine in Rome, built in the early fourth century

❖ JOHN NASH (1752–1835) ❖

John Nash was probably born in London, though his parents were in fact Welsh. He was employed as a teenager in the office of the architect Robert Taylor, coming into contact with some of the very best buildings of the day. His first attempt to establish himself independently ended in disaster: declared bankrupt in 1783, he moved to Wales. There he emerged as the leading architect of the Picturesque, and in 1796 he returned to London, working for a while in successful partnership with the fashionable landscape-gardener, Humphry Repton.

In 1806 Nash was appointed architect to the Office of Woods and Forests, in which capacity he found growing royal favour. From 1811 onwards, his was the brilliance which lay behind the

Portrait of John Nash by Sir Thomas Lawrence

master plan for Regent's Park and Regent Street, schemes which brought the notion of the Picturesque to the town. Nash was now as much innovative town planner as he was architect. Around the park itself, he designed extraordinary terraces with palatial façades rendered in stucco, including Park Crescent,

Chester Terrace, and Cumberland Terrace.

In 1813 Nash was appointed the Regent's Surveyor General, and it was as the prince's personal architect that he began remodelling the Royal Pavilion in Brighton in 1815. Ten years later, with George now king, and Regent Street almost complete, Nash was handed the Buckingham Palace commission. He was already 73, and it was an ill-starred venture from the start. As the bitter row over costs escalated, Nash became the butt of public displeasure. He was eventually sacked, his reputation left in shreds. Nash spent much of his last years at his country seat of East Cowes Castle on the Isle of Wight. There he died in 1835, a very old and tired man, and was buried in the local churchyard.

was fast becoming an object of contempt: Thomas Creevey MP pronounced it 'the Devil's own'. For all this, Nash was effectively vindicated in a Select Committee report of 1828, and the work moved forward.

Meanwhile, Flaxman's death in 1826 had left the question of the sculpture unresolved. Not until June

1828 were contracts agreed with three other eminent sculptors. The bulk of the commission, including the two friezes in high relief on the long sides, was given to Richard Westmacott. Other elements were offered to Edward Hodges Baily, and one of the attic plinth groups went to Charles Rossi. The king also persuaded Francis Chantrey to take on his equestrian statue for the summit of the arch, though Chantrey insisted in working in bronze rather than marble.

By the early summer of 1830 the body of the arch was almost finished up to the level of the cornice. The fluted columns and their capitals were in place, and virtually all of the carved panels and figures were awaiting erection. Behind this positive front, however, much else was in utter chaos. Soon after the king's death in June, the Treasury ordered that building on the palace and the arch was to be suspended. Nash himself was effectively sacked in October, and the following year another Select Committee looked into the financial administration of the works as a whole. It concluded, albeit reluctantly, that the only sensible course of action was to complete the building as expediently and cheaply as possible.

The responsibility was given to Edward Blore, an architect who came with something of a reputation for cut-price success. Though his work was generally competent, if rather dull in character, his contributions to Buckingham Palace were far from satisfactory. The Marble Arch was to come off particularly badly. Blore recommended it should be finished much as it stood, without the attic pedestal and equestrian statue. The lower it is kept, he argued, 'the better it will look and the less it will interfere with the Palace'. He got his way. Much of the sculpture was disregarded, and the arch was completed in its sadly reduced form in 1832–33.

Thereafter, the Marble Arch stood as a formal gateway at the east front of Buckingham Palace for seventeen years. The great central gates, designed by Nash and fabricated by Samuel Parker, were finally hung in place in time for the accession of Queen Victoria in 1837, and a year later it was through the arch that her coronation procession set out for Westminster Abbey.

The south face of the Marble Arch

MISSING SCULPTURE
FROM THE MARBLE ARCH

❖   ❖

As a consequence of John Flaxman's death in 1826, Nash eventually turned to Richard Westmacott (d 1856), E H Baily (d 1867) and Charles Rossi (d 1839) to execute the projected sculptural decoration for his Marble Arch. Two allegorical panels by Westmacott and two more by Baily were in fact used, as were their keystones and Victory figures around the arches. However, Blore's unfortunate economies left the vast bulk of the material without specific purpose, totally undermining the commemorative role which had been envisaged for the arch.

In the event, Blore was to take two-thirds of Westmacott's long Waterloo frieze and two of his Nelson panels from the other principal façade, using them in the east front of the palace itself. He also positioned Westmacott's reliefs intended for either end of the arch on the west or garden front of the palace. Other pieces were happily taken by William Wilkins for the

Relief showing Nelson accepting the Spanish surrender after the battle of St Vincent in 1797

new National Gallery, begun in 1833. Hence, Baily's attic plinth Britannia (modified to represent Minerva) found a home on the east side of the building, whereas

Rossi's group for the opposite side of the arch plinth, representing Europe and Asia, was placed over the main entrance to the gallery.

Remarkable though it seems, two long-lost sections of the Marble Arch reliefs surfaced in 1985 from an outhouse at Shepperton Film Studios. One is definitely by Westmacott, showing Napoleon's retreat from the field at Waterloo. The other, probably by Westmacott, depicts Nelson accepting the Spanish surrender after the battle of St Vincent (1797). First auctioned in 1985, the pieces were resold ten years later, and the Nelson panel appeared in auction once again in 1999.

Perhaps the most striking of all the Marble Arch sculpture was Chantrey's glorious bronze equestrian statue of George IV. It was left without a home until 1843, when it was given 'temporary occupation' on one of two new plinths in Trafalgar Square. It has remained there ever since.

The statue of George IV in Trafalgar Square by Francis Chantrey

The removal to Cumberland Gate: 1850–51

The possibility of removing the Marble Arch from the front of Buckingham Palace altogether was first raised as early as 1833. Blore advised against such action on grounds of cost, and for the time being it was left alone. The situation was to become very different in the 1840s. Queen Victoria found that the palace was far too small for her household, and in 1845 she wrote to the Prime Minister on 'the urgent necessity of doing something' about it. Blore's solution was to build a new east wing, making a nonsense of Nash's open courtyard design, and bringing the Marble Arch far too close to the now extended palace façade. This absurd situation dragged on until the spring of 1850, when something finally had to be done.

Decimus Burton and W A Nesfield had been appointed to plan the palace forecourt and environs. In June they presented an estimate which included a sum for the removal and rebuilding of the arch. Two months later, Thomas Cubitt, the contractor for the palace works at large, tendered £700 for taking apart the arch and laying it out in an enclosure in Green Park. By the end of October it was down, every block numbered so that they could be reassembled elsewhere. There was no shortage of suggestions for the new site, but in the end

Burton and Nesfield decided that it should go to Cumberland Gate, at the north-east corner of Hyde Park.

In the first week of 1851, Cubitt began preparing the site. The works progressed rapidly, often extending late into the night under the illumination of gaslights. In the process of rebuilding, Cubitt was instructed to make various modifications to the design, notably the conversion of the three interior chambers to 'living rooms'. When, at the end of March, the work was complete, *The Times* thought the arch presented an altogether 'very chaste appearance'. Within weeks, crowds of people would flock by it on their way into Hyde Park for the Great Exhibition.

Nash designed splendid ornamental gates for the arch and commissioned Samuel Parker to make them. When work was halted on the palace and the arch in 1830, the gates remained unfinished. The pieces were finally assembled by the firm of Bramah and Prestage in 1837

Left: one of the gate roundels depicting St George and the dragon

So it was that the Marble Arch arrived in its present position. As planned by Burton and Nesfield, the arch would form a grand ceremonial entrance into the park, corresponding with Burton's screen at Hyde Park Corner. Low iron gates for daily use were placed on either side, and just to the west Burton's little gate lodge of the 1820s was rebuilt as part of the scheme. The arch was to enjoy this role for almost sixty years, eventually giving its name to the immediate area, as well as to the local underground station.

The Marble Arch today

When it was erected at Cumberland Gate in 1851, the orientation of the Marble Arch was turned through some 90 degrees. The triple-arched long axis now runs east to west, whereas at Buckingham Palace it had stood north to south. Hence, what is now the outer

From 1851 to 1908 the Marble Arch served as a grand entrance to Hyde Park: this view dates from about 1900

face (overlooking the busy Oxford Street and Bayswater Road junction) was to have been the military or Waterloo side of the arch, that originally approached on entering the palace. The façade which now looks south over the open square was intended as the naval or Trafalgar side.

Up to the principal cornice, the design can be wholly attributed to John Nash. The stunted attic, naked without its sculpture and broken only with crude inverted consoles, is Blore's unhappy compromise. Despite the chequered history reflected in this broad split, the arch remains a striking piece of architecture. Some of the imperial grandeur intended for it by Nash has been restored since its marble was cleaned and polished in 1994 and again, extensively, in 2004.

Each of the eight massive fluted columns is cut from a monolithic slab of marble, with their capitals modelled on Roman examples. Samuel Parker's superb 'mosaic gold' (a form of bronze) gates hang in the centre arch, whereas the gates in the side arches originated with a suggestion from Blore, later modified by Thomas Cubitt. At either end, beneath the three laurel wreaths, there were to have been naval and military inscriptions, in low bronze relief. On the present southern façade, the six Victories in the spandrels of the arches are all by Baily; so too are the relief panels, both of which are allegorical scenes

Relief panel on the north side of the arch, showing Peace holding an olive branch above the trophies of war

Relief panel on the south side, showing Peace and Plenty

in neo-classical style. In the panel to the left a naval warrior is depicted with the figure of Justice; in that to the right the two female figures represent Peace and Plenty. On the north side of the arch, the carving is all by Westmacott. The panel to the left is a personification of England, flanked by Wales and Scotland; that to the right is the semi-nude female figure of Peace, standing above the trophies of war.

THE ARCHES IN THE TWENTIETH CENTURY

E ven before 1900, Marble Arch and Hyde Park Corner were notorious for their traffic jams. Then, in 1905, a Royal Commission on London Traffic discovered that more than 29,000 vehicles passed the

Marble Arch in a single day. It proved a disastrous statistic for the fate of the monument: three years later a London County Council road improvement scheme left the Marble Arch marooned on a tiny island,

Hyde Park Corner, about 1930

© CROWN COPYRIGHT. NMR

The Marble Arch after 1908 on its small traffic island, entirely separated from Hyde Park

❖ THE POLICE AND THE ARCHES ❖

A significant aspect to the history of the arches is that for many years they served as the two smallest police stations in London. In the case of the Wellington Arch, the police shared the occupation of the building with the park gate-keeper from as early as 1831. They were obliged to vacate their accommodation in time for the removal of the arch in 1882, but by April 1884 all was ready for an inspector and fifteen constables to move back. Over at the Marble Arch, Thomas Cubitt had been instructed to convert the interior spaces to 'living rooms' during the rebuilding early in 1851. Before the end of the year,

PUBLIC RECORD OFFICE

Sergeant Cecil Pollard and Snooks the cat in the Wellington Arch, 1952

the Chief Commissioner of police had requested that the building should be available to the force for carrying on its duties in Hyde Park. The rooms would afford accommodation for six single men, he thought, whilst in times of commotion the arch 'would admit

a considerable body of Police being assembled at this important point'.

Indeed, from the time of the Great Exhibition in 1851, the managing of large crowds in the park was to become of increasing concern to the police. In 1866–67, a former military barracks near the centre of the park was converted for the use of the force, and this was replaced in 1902 by a purpose-built Metropolitan Police station. The Marble Arch meanwhile continued to serve as a useful outpost, and the Wellington Arch was for long a 'section house', its officers mainly concerned with the policing of the area around Constitution Hill and to the south of Hyde Park Corner.

This page: restoration work in progress on the Wellington Arch

Opposite: an aerial view of Hyde Park Corner with the Wellington Arch (centre), Apsley House (left) and the Hyde Park Screen (lower centre)

severed completely from the park entrance. The rising volume of traffic eventually called for yet more drastic action, in the shape of the Park Lane widening scheme, carried out in 1960–62. This alleviated the problem, but at a very high cost. The broad new highway cut a swathe from Hyde Park, and separated it from Mayfair. Huge roundabouts were created at Marble Arch and Hyde Park Corner, further isolating the arches and destroying their fine architectural settings of gates, piers and railings.

Between 1999 and 2000 the creation of level pedestrian crossings at Hyde Park Corner and the establishment of the Princess Diana Memorial Walk revitalized the Wellington Arch island as a route from Hyde Park to Green Park. Moreover, in 1999 English Heritage took on responsibility for the long-term care of both arches. The still luminous qualities in the Ravaccione fabric of the Marble Arch were revealed in an external restoration in 1994.

The Wellington Arch, though, was in poor condition, and a £1.5 million repair project was carried out in 1999–2000. This included cleaning and repair of the masonry, and works to reinforce the broad lintels over the two main openings, ensuring their safety. Layers of old blackened lanolin wax were cleaned off Adrian Jones's quadriga, which was newly patinated and waxed. The gates were

cleaned, and repainted in a bronze green, close to their original colour. The arch was adapted for public access, with viewing platforms created over the porticoes and exhibition spaces inside, with the aim of increasing public appreciation and enjoyment of the two arches, and of London's wider heritage of public statues and monuments.

Hyde Park Corner from the east, showing the Wellington Arch, with the Hyde Park Screen, Boehm's statue of Wellington and Apsley House in the background

Further reading

Dana Arnold, 'The Arch at Constitution Hill: A New Axis for London', *Apollo*, **138**, No. 379 (1993), 129–33.

Steven Brindle, 'The Wellington Arch, Hyde Park Corner, and the Idea of a Western Entrance to London', *The Georgian Group Journal*, **11** (2001), 47–92.

Howard Colvin, *A Biographical Dictionary of British Architects 1600–1840*, 4th edition (New Haven and London 2008).

J Mordaunt Crook and M H Port, *The History of the King's Works: Volume VI, 1782–1851* (London 1973).

Adrian Jones, *Memoirs of a Soldier Artist* (London 1933).

John Physick, *The Wellington Memorial* (London 1970).

Andrew Saint, 'The Marble Arch', *The Georgian Group Journal*, **7** (1997), 75–93.

H Clifford Smith, 'Vicissitudes of the Marble Arch', *Country Life*, **112** (1952), 38–39.

John Summerson, *The Life and Work of John Nash, Architect* (London 1980).

Margaret Whinney, *Sculpture in Britain 1530 to 1830*, 2nd edition, revised by John Physick (London 1988).